D0536775

ATEN BY A SHARK

Sue Hamilton

VISIT US AT
WWW.ABDOPUBLISHING.COM

Published by ABDO Publishing Company, 8000 West 78th Street, Suite 310, Edina, MN 55439. Copyright ©2010 by Abdo Consulting Group, Inc. International copyrights reserved in all countries. No part of this book may be reproduced in any form without written permission from the publisher. ABDO & Daughters™ is a trademark and logo of ABDO Publishing Company.

Printed in the United States of America, North Mankato, Minnesota
112009
012010

♲ PRINTED ON RECYCLED PAPER

Editor & Graphic Design: John Hamilton
Cover Design: John Hamilton
Cover Photo: Getty Images
Interior Photos and Illustrations: AP Images, p. 20; Corbis, p. 7, 8, 9, 28; Getty Images, p. 4, 5, 11, 13, 14, 18, 23, 27, 29; iStockphoto, p. 1, 3, 6, 16, 17, 19, 21, 25, 32; National Geographic, p. 12; Photo Researchers, p. 10, 15, 26; Visuals Unlimited, p. 22, 24.

Library of Congress Cataloging-in-Publication Data

Hamilton, Sue L., 1959-
  Eaten by a shark / Sue Hamilton.
      p. cm. -- (Close encounters of the wild kind)
  Includes index.
  ISBN 978-1-60453-931-8
  1. Shark attacks--Juvenile literature. 2. Sharks--Juvenile literature. I. Title.
  QL638.93.H36 2010
  597.3--dc22
                    2009037230

CONTENTS

PREDATORS OF THE SEA

Just seeing a shark's dorsal fin above the water can send waves of terror into swimmers, divers, and surfers. Humans are wise to respect these powerful predators of the sea. There are about 400 different shark species, and nature has provided these fish with the killing tools needed for survival. Some species have swum the earth's oceans for more than 400 million years.

Sharks have rows of sharp, pointed, death-dealing teeth. And sharks never run out of them. When one tooth falls out, another comes in. A shark may go through as many as 20,000 teeth during its lifetime.

Sharp teeth are important, but how a shark uses them is the key to its success as a predator. When a shark bites down, it shakes its prey back and forth, allowing its serrated teeth to act like miniature saws. Sharks can chomp through a human's arm or leg with ease. And if razor-sharp teeth aren't enough, sharks also have superior eyesight, hearing, and smell.

Right: A great white shark inspects a diver taking photos from inside a safety cage.
Facing page: A great white shark rears up from the water.

SHARK SENSES

Sharks' eyes, ears, and noses are designed to help them find prey. Their eyesight is keen in the water, and it's believed they may even see above the waterline. Sharks can hear prey from as far away as 700 feet (213 m). For example, if a 57-story skyscraper was filled with water, a person splashing at the top could be heard by a shark swimming at the bottom.

Sharks' noses can detect even a few drops of blood in the water. Blood molecules travel quickly with the help of ocean currents. Sharks may pick up this smell from a mile (1.6 km) or more away. Their sleek, muscle-powered frames move swiftly through the water, swimming up to 31 miles per hour (50 km/hr) to the source of the smell.

Above: A shark uses its keen senses to find prey.
Facing page: A great white shark is attracted to bloody chum dumped into the water.

Sharks even have an extra gland in their body that detects electromagnetic signals given off by living creatures. This helps sharks pinpoint the exact location of their prey.

People rightfully fear these mighty predators, but in reality they are more likely to be struck by a coconut falling on their head. In fact, sharks don't even much like the taste of humans. Most people are attacked because sharks think they are going after their favorite meals, which includes seals or sea turtles.

But even though shark attacks on humans are infrequent, they do happen. Some people are killed. Others survive to tell their traumatic tales of the moments when they were eaten by a shark.

Above: From below, surfers or boaters with hands and feet dangling in the water resemble seals or sea turtles, a shark's favorite foods.

BULL SHARK DANGER

On May 6, 2009, vacationer Luis Hernandez was spearfishing in the beautiful waters of the Bahamas. Hernandez had just speared a grouper, when a bull shark turned the fisherman into the "catch."

Bull sharks are a species that is often involved in attacks on humans. This may be because bull sharks live in warm, shallow tropical waters of 100 feet (30 m) or less. They can even survive for a period of time in freshwater, traveling up rivers, bays, and harbors. These habitats, not surprisingly, lead to frequent contact with humans. And bull sharks are not picky eaters. They'd prefer to eat other fish, but they will dine on almost anything, including people.

Named "bull sharks" because of their stub-nosed snouts, these fish are often seen cruising slowly across the ocean floor. But don't be fooled. When prey presents itself, a bull shark is fast and aggressive, and it has a broad jaw filled with rows of serrated teeth designed to quickly grab its next meal.

Right: A bull shark bites down on its next meal.
Facing page: Like most sharks, bull sharks have a mouthful of sharp, serrated teeth.

"All of a sudden, it felt as though a torpedo hit my body."

—Luis Hernandez, May 6, 2009, Exuma Islands, Bahamas

Luis Hernandez discovered the ferocity of a bull shark on that May morning. He had seen the bull shark cruising near him. He tried poking it to persuade it to leave. Instead, the shark turned and attacked, biting down on Hernandez's arm and holding on tight. "I tried to fight him, I'm gonna say for about 30 seconds, and finally got him off my arm. And I injured my other hand trying to open his jaw," said Hernandez.

In seconds, a chunk of the fisherman's forearm was gone, exposing his bone. Blood filled the water.

Above: A close-up photograph of a bull shark's teeth.

Hernandez credits his wife with saving his life. Marlene Hernandez saw what had happened, and immediately raised anchor and moved their boat next to her traumatized husband. She managed to pull him into the boat and get back to shore. Hernandez was brought to a local hospital, and then airlifted to a hospital in Miami, Florida. He underwent several surgeries on his mangled arm, but he lived.

It is likely that the bull shark wanted the grouper that Hernandez had speared. The blood in the water from the fish may have provoked the attack. Or perhaps when Hernandez poked at the shark, it tried to protect itself. Either way, in this shark vs. human encounter, Hernandez was lucky that the shark only made off with a chunk of his arm, and not with his life.

Above: A bull shark cruises the warm waters off the Bahama Islands.

GREAT WHITE ATTACK

On a beautiful, clear California day in 1993, David Miles took a day off work to go diving for abalone with three friends. He never thought that this dive might nearly cost him his life.

Great white sharks were made famous in the 1970s by Peter Benchley's novel and the subsequent movie, *Jaws*. In this story, a monstrous great white shark attacks and kills swimmers, fishermen, and even pets. In reality, however, great whites are somewhat picky eaters. They like seals, fish, sea lions, elephant seals, and small toothed whales. Many of these tasty shark treats are found in the waters off California's shores. Great whites, however, do not care much for the taste of humans. And that may be what saved David Miles.

Right: Despite how great white sharks are depicted in *Jaws* and other stories, these predators are actually more interested in eating fish and seals than humans.

Great white shark

"I thought my skull was being crushed."
—David Miles, August 12, 1993, Westport Union Landing State Beach, California

Miles had just started to swim to the surface from the ocean floor when the shark struck. "I was slammed... it felt like a bus had hit me," he said. Miles had just experienced the great white's "ambush" hunting style. Their mottled grey coloring blends in with their surroundings, which helps great whites speed undetected toward their prey from below.

Seconds after being struck, David Miles was halfway down the shark's mouth. Miles was surrounded by rows of razor-sharp, serrated teeth biting down on his head and shoulders. He did the only thing he could—he fought back, striking at the great predator. The shark spit Miles out. Perhaps it realized the diver wasn't its normal prey, or maybe Miles' wet suit left a bad taste in the shark's mouth. Said Miles, "When he opened his mouth back up again, that was my window of opportunity to escape."

Above: A great white shark rises to take bait from a boat near Dyer Island, South Africa.

Bleeding from his head and shoulders, Miles swam to a rock and pulled himself up, calling to his friends to get out of the water. They did, but after seeing Miles' injuries, they knew they'd have to return to the water to get Miles to a hospital.

Miraculously, everyone made it safely back to shore. Miles was flown by helicopter to a local hospital. He required more than 100 stitches to close the wounds on his back, scalp, and jaw. Some experts estimate there is a 300-million-to-one chance of surviving a great white attack. Stated Miles, "I felt like I won the lottery that day."

Above: A great white shark seen near Guadalupe Island, Mexico.

A TIGER'S BITE

As she did most days, 13-year-old Bethany Hamilton went surfing on Halloween morning 2003. When the young, award-winning surfer arrived back at the beach, she had only one arm, and half her body's blood was in the ocean.

Named for their dark, tiger-like stripes, tiger sharks are found near coastlines in the warmer waters of the Pacific and Atlantic Oceans. Their preferred habitat keeps them in frequent contact with surfers, swimmers, and divers. These encounters and easy identification have resulted in tiger sharks earning the status as the shark species with the second-most recorded attacks on humans. (Only the great white shark has more.)

Above: A tiger shark feeds on a young albatross.

Tiger shark

Surfers constantly share the ocean with sharks and other sea creatures. Bethany Hamilton, who began surfing when she was five years old, had spent thousands of hours in the ocean waters surrounding her Hawaii home. Early on the morning of October 31, 2003, she accompanied her friend Alana Blanchard and Alana's father and brother to a surfing spot known as The Tunnels. Paddling out about ¼ mile (.4 km), Bethany and Alana were on their surfboards, waiting for a wave. Bethany lay on her board with her left arm dangling in the water. Without warning, a tiger shark leapt up from the water, biting Bethany's arm, along with a chunk of her surfboard. With a shake of its powerful head, the tiger shark severed Hamilton's arm up to her shoulder, then slid back into the water.

Bleeding heavily, but without panicking, Bethany called to her friends. A surfboard leash was used as a tourniquet to stop the bleeding, and all three managed to get her back to the beach. Rushed to the local hospital, immediate blood transfusions and emergency surgery saved the young surfer's life. Within weeks, Bethany was back in the water, learning to surf with only one arm. Her bravery and positive attitude made her an international sensation. Today, she continues to competitively surf, but she is smarter when it comes to sharks.

Right: Bethany Hamilton competing in a National Scholastic Surfing Association meet in Hawaii. Even after losing her arm to a tiger shark, she was back on her surfboard after only a few weeks.

> # "I looked down at the water and it was, like, really red from all the blood..."
> —Bethany Hamilton, October 31, 2003, Kauai, Hawaii

Tiger sharks feed in the mornings and evenings—a time when many surfers stay out of the water, especially if sharks have been spotted. Tiger sharks love to eat sea turtles. Before the attack, Bethany was lying on her light-colored surfboard with her arm in the water. To a shark lurking in the depths, she could easily have been mistaken for a tasty turtle snack. Today, Bethany prefers a surfboard with dark stripes, which resembles a poisonous sea creature that sharks do not like.

As for the tiger shark, local fisherman Ralph Young caught a 1,400 pound (635 kg) tiger shark within days of the attack. Young stated, "When we took the outline of the bite in the board, and compared it to the jaws that I've got, it fits perfectly."

Above: Divers film a tiger shark off Australia's Great Barrier Reef.

NURSE SHARKS

Nurse sharks are bottom feeders. They use their pharynx, a muscle-lined cavity behind their nose and mouth, to powerfully suck up fish, crustaceans (lobsters, crabs, and shrimp), and mollusks (octopi, squid, and clams). Nurse sharks often don't even use their small mouths or teeth to eat. They just vacuum up their food from the ocean floor.

Nurse sharks usually feed at night. During the day, the sluggish fish rest in holes and rocky crevices. They are a familiar sight in the shallow waters off the eastern and southern coasts of the United States, especially Florida. Many attacks by slow nurse sharks have been due to people attempting to feed the sharks or grab their tails. Like most wild animals when disturbed or threatened, nurse sharks protect themselves. In September 2007, 14-year-old Brendan Chapman discovered this firsthand.

Above: A nurse shark rests in the Sugar Wreck, the remains of an old sailing ship that sank off the coast of the Bahamas in the Atlantic Ocean.

A nurse shark in the Caribbean waters off Belize.

"The shark is still attached."

—Lt. Rob Melendez, referring to an emergency call he received regarding Brendan Chapman, September 13, 2007, Lauderdale-by-the-Sea, Florida

The Florida Museum of Natural History writes about nurse sharks: "If disturbed, it may bite with a powerful vice-like grip capable of inflicting serious injury. In some instances, jaw release was accomplished only after using surgical instruments." While snorkeling in the ocean near Lauderdale-by-the-Sea, Florida, Brendan Chapman ended up with a 4-foot (1.2-m) nurse shark locked onto his stomach. Even after walking out of the water, the teen could not get the stubborn nurse shark to let go.

Above: A nurse shark cruising over a reef in the Indian Ocean.

On the beach, rescuers poked and jabbed at the nurse shark, desperately trying to make the fish open its jaws without further hurting the boy. Finally, Lt. Rob Melendez of the Broward Sheriff's Fire Rescue arrived. "I just gave him a big nudge in the nose, like a pound in the nose," stated Melendez. "He kind of shook his body. And he let go."

The nurse shark was returned to the ocean. Chapman ended his day at a nearby medical center. While his wound was minor, he discovered that even an easy-going shark is still a powerful predator.

Above: A diver plays with a nurse shark by rubbing its belly. Although they are often docile, nurse sharks can be unpredictable, like any wild animal.

SURVIVING AN ATTACK

The International Shark Attack File (ISAF) tracks shark attacks around the world. The ISAF states, "Worldwide, there are probably 70 to 100 shark attacks annually, resulting in about 5 to 15 deaths." A person is more likely to be killed from fireworks than from an attack by the millions of sharks in the world's oceans. Sharks, however, are not so lucky.

For every person a shark kills, 10 million sharks are killed by humans. Many shark species have been hunted nearly to extinction. The oceans need these great predators to keep the sea's ecology in balance. Julia Baum, a fisheries biologist, studied the impact on the United States East Coast of large sharks being killed off. Baum reported, "With fewer sharks around, the species they prey upon—like cownose rays—have increased in numbers, and in turn, hordes of cownose rays dining on bay scallops have wiped the scallops out." The bottom line is that the earth needs sharks.

Above: Feet dangling in the water makes a tempting meal for a shark. Although the thought of being attacked by a shark is very frightening, the fact is that humans are the ones doing the most killing. In fact, several shark species have been so over-hunted that they have been pushed nearly to extinction.

Though rare, shark attacks are very real, and the United States has the most of any country. So, other than never entering the ocean, what can be done to survive a shark attack? First, try not to be attacked! Pay attention to your surroundings. The great white, tiger shark, and bull shark are the species most likely to attack humans. If you are swimming, surfing, or diving in areas where these or other sharks live, stay out of the water during early morning, dusk, or evening hours, when sharks are most active. Also, stay away from deep dropoffs where sharks feed.

A lone swimmer is more likely to be attacked than a group of swimmers. However, sharks are attracted to splashing, brightly colored swimwear, and shiny watches, rings, and bracelets, all of which sound and look like fish dinner to hungry sharks. They can smell blood in the water from even a small cut. If you have a recent wound, protect yourself and others by simply staying out of the water.

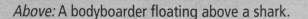

Above: A bodyboarder floating above a shark.

Even if all the rules are followed, you may still find yourself face-to-face with one of these powerful predators. If you are attacked, fight back. Repeatedly and quickly strike the shark's eyes or gills. It may be fooled into thinking many attackers are after it. Use anything available to hit the shark—a camera, or an oar, for example.

It's commonly believed that a shark attack on a human is really a case of mistaken identity. Once a shark realizes you are not a tasty sea turtle or seal, it may spit you out and swim off. However, even a brief encounter often leaves people with large, bleeding gashes. Blood in the water can excite the shark to continue attacking, or the blood could easily attract other sharks to the area, causing a feeding frenzy. Calmly and quickly get out of the water, apply pressure to stop the bleeding, and seek medical help immediately. Most people survive shark attacks, but everyone should learn to respect these predators of the sea.

Above: Sharks can attack even in shallow water. Be aware of your surroundings.

GLOSSARY

ABALONE
An edible shell creature that lives in warm waters, such as the Pacific Ocean. It is distinguished by its ear-shaped shell.

AGILE
Able to move fast.

AMBUSH
A surprise attack by someone or something hiding nearby.

BAHAMAS
Also called the Bahama Islands. A country of many islands located southeast of Florida in the Atlantic Ocean. The Bahamas are a popular tourist destination, and known for good diving.

DORSAL FIN
The large main fin that is on the back of many fish, including sharks. It is sometimes seen above the water when a fish swims close to the surface.

ELECTROMAGNETIC SIGNALS
Living things give off an invisible, electrical magnetic force. Some creatures, such as sharks, have senses that can detect these signals. This allows sharks to locate living things, even if the shark can't immediately see its prey.

EXTINCT

When there are no more living species of a certain plant or animal. Dinosaurs are now extinct. In modern times, the dodo bird is an example of an animal whose extinction was caused by humans. Many shark species are in danger of extinction because of over-hunting by people.

FEROCITY

The act of being fierce, strong, and powerful.

MOLECULE

The smallest amount of a substance that still keeps the physical and chemical composition of the substance.

MOTTLED

Spots and patches of color that are different sizes and shapes.

PREDATOR

An animal that preys on other animals.

SERRATED

Notched like the edge of a saw. Many species of sharks have jagged, serrated teeth, which allows them to rip off big chunks of meat.

TRAUMATIZE

A terrifying or shocking experience that may cause both mental and physical injuries to the victim.

INDEX

Above: A great white shark.